One New Fix Your Marriage

10 Simple Steps To Put The Joy And Intimacy Back In Your Marriage

Grace Stevens

Copyright © 2013 Grace Stevens - Red Lotus Books

All rights reserved.   No part of this book may be reproduced in any form without permission in writing from the author. Reviewers may quote brief passages in reviews.

Published by Red Lotus Books, Mountain House CA

website: http://www.OneNewHabit.com

http://www.GraceStevens.com

Claim Your Free Gift!

As a special "thank you" for buying my book you can get immediate access to an exclusive eCourse by Top Relationship Coach Mort Fertel. This ecourse is based on the hugely successful Marriage Fitness Program that has over 1 million satisfied subscribers.

For a limited time you can access the eCourse and 5 exclusive Marriage Assessments.

Visit the One New Habit website at www.OneNewHabit.com and click the "Marriage gift" tab

"http://OneNewHabit/marriage-gift"

Table of Contents

Why One New Habit?

Are you currently living the marriage of your dreams, or your nightmares? I'm guessing neither. More likely you are living a "hum-ho" version of marriage that is somewhere in between - a version sometimes referred to as "Management Incorporated" where your once sacred relationship has deteriorated to a polite (or not so polite) business partnership and delegation of shared duties and responsibilities.

Do you long to be happier, less stressed, more organized and have more rewarding personal relationships? Do you want to get the passion back in your life and your marriage? I sure did.

Let me introduce myself. I'm Grace. I'm a self development nerd. (Note, I say "nerd", not "junkie"...that word has too many bad associations as any self respecting self development nerd would know). My idea of a great night in is a couple of great TED talk videos on neuro-science and a glass of wine. Let Elizabeth Gilbert go off globe trotting for a year to "find herself" while eating, praying and loving. (Really, most of us can barely conceive of taking a weekend or even a night off.) You and I ...we can get enlightenment right here, right now. Well, you can. I actually spent 2 decades and a lot of money on books, courses, seminars, therapists and spiritual "gurus" with the goal of giving my life an "overhaul". Here's the GREAT NEWS for you. I didn't need to. And neither do you!

Bottom line -what 20 plus years of research, meditating and personal growth has taught me is this...it all boils down to the 80/20 rule - in improving your relationships and your life, 80% of the results come from just 20% of the actions.

The One New Habit book series is about that 20% of actions.

This book series is aimed at giving you a manageable sized book that you CAN realistically finish reading. You can read it on your Kindle, your phone or your laptop at your convenience on the go. The series will provide you with simple, easy strategies that can apply TODAY in YOUR life. The easy 20% that can make a huge difference. All for less than the price of a fancy cup of coffee.

So can you do all of the 10 things in this book today? Well, it's unlikely that you will do them all. But the fact is that there is NOT ONE of the action items that you COULDN'T do today, if you wanted to. None of these are strategies that require a lot of time or financial resources. Commit to doing one thing today. And then tomorrow pick another thing to do. Keep working on these actions daily until they become habits. If a couple of the strategies don't appeal to you, don't sweat it. Just get started with something and see where it takes you!

Let's get started!

Chapter 1 - Time To Rip Up The Score Sheet

So are you married to a complete jerk, or a total witch?

Probably not. I'm guessing that your spouse's goal when they get up in the morning is not to irritate, exasperate, belittle, abuse and under appreciate you (even if it sometimes feels that way). Your spouse is probably not relishing the current reality of your marriage any more than you are (although there is a very strong possibility that they are pretty ambivalent or apathetic about it).

Some marriages face some very difficult circumstances and trying to save these marriages is not advisable. These would include marriages where the following are present... we'll call them:

DEAL BREAKERS

Physical or Emotional Abuse (of you or your children)

Violence of any kind

Drug or Alcohol Abuse

Other Addiction Issues (gambling, pornography, sex)

Chronic Adultery (repeated affairs as opposed to a "slip up" or "cry for help" affair)

You have to be honest and ask yourself if these are the realities of your current situation. If they are, I am REALLY sorry. But please recognize that this book is not for you. Seriously. You need to seek professional help and support and get out of your marriage. Not all marriages can or even should be saved. Abuse is NEVER acceptable and it is never your fault. In these circumstances your goal should not be to save or fix your marriage, but to get out of it safely. Please seriously think about this and get the support you need from family and professionals if you are dealing with any of these issues.

Realistically, the above issues account for a very small percentage of marriages that fail. In most cases there is nothing as dramatic as abuse that ends a marriage. Most marriages wither away from neglect of one sort or another. Even in cases when there is an extra marital affair, most people recognize that affairs don't happen in a vacuum - they are usually set against a backdrop of a troubled marriage.

So this book IS for you if any of the following scenarios sound painfully familiar.

We'll call these:

SYMPTOMS OF A DETERIORATING MARRIAGE

- You are tired of hearing "I love you but I'm not in love with you"

- You find yourself avoiding physical intimacy with your spouse, or alternatively you are frustrated that your spouse is avoiding being physically intimate with you

- You rarely share quality "alone" time with your spouse

- You find your relationship feels more like a business partnership of convenience or a "room mate" type situation than a passionate marriage

- You have increasing stress involving finances. You hide purchases or money from your spouse

- You or your spouse avoid dealing with your relationship problems by over eating, over working, over exercising or finding other excuses to be out of the house

- Your communication with your spouse is primarily through texts, notes, bickering or relaying messages through your children. Your relationship has deteriorated to a delegation of tasks and responsibilities

- You are sleeping in separate rooms or regularly go to bed at different times

- One of you has expressed interest or the need for marital counseling but the other one is reluctant to participate

- You fantasize about what it would be like to be alone or in a relationship with someone else

- You are dealing with or suspect that you are dealing with your spouse either having a physical or emotional affair

These are all symptoms of a marriage at risk of just dying from neglect. The age old "we just stopped trying".

The good news is that there are MANY things you can do to turn the tide of your marriage. Even if your spouse is uninterested in counseling (really, who wants to go air out their past grievances and "dirty laundry" in front of a stranger, anyway?) there are still steps you can take that can improve the quality of your marriage.

But the VERY first step here is to examine your mindset and work with this idea :

It is going to be easier to change your mindset than to change your mate.

The essential truth of any relationship is this - your contribution, from an emotional standpoint at least, is 50%. That's half. You make up half of the marriage. If you are truly interested in having a happier, healthier marriage then the first step is to acknowledge this fact.

There are probably many areas in which your spouse could improve. No doubt there are countless things that your spouse does or does not do on a daily basis that drive you crazy. But experience by now has probably taught you that you cannot really control how another person acts. Only they can control that. Seriously, have any of the annoying habits you have nagged your spouse about ever changed? What you can control is what you think and feel and how you act.

Theoretically, if you can totally control 50% of the marriage then the marriage has a chance of being 50% better. This is true even if your spouse is in denial that there is a problem, or seems apathetic about wanting to fix it. Please understand that my goal here is not to delegate blame and insinuate that 50% of the problems in your marriage are of your making! My goal here is to empower you.

At this point I would assume that improving your marriage by 50% sounds pretty good. But there's more. What many people have found that is if you control the things you can control, if you can focus on changing your thoughts, feelings and actions, then the energy in the marriage will most likely change. Once the energy or "tone" of your marriage changes the improvement will not be just 50%, but actually has the potential to make a quantum leap.

So step one is pretty simple. (Note, I said "simple" not "easy"). Step one is to acknowledge that you are 50% of the marriage and that you have the ability to change your thoughts, feelings and actions within your marriage.

Now I'm guessing here that some of you are having the initial gut reaction of "why should I be the one to change my behavior?" Many deteriorating marriages find themselves in a place where there are a series of bad relationship habits from both parties, a lot of resentments built up and a lot of "score keeping" (more on that in a minute). It's like a big stalemate or giant game of "chicken" to see who will cave and make the first conciliatory move. Please think about that for a minute and reflect if any of that sounds applicable to your current situation. It may sound like a cliche, but it is actually true that there is no prize in life for being unhappily married. You should be the one to change because you want to have a happier, more loving, supportive and relaxed marriage. Someone has to make the first move. In fact you ALREADY made the first move when you downloaded this book. Good job!

Again, many couples have found that once one partner takes positive, proactive steps to improve a marriage the other partner, enjoying the new energy and tone of the marriage, just gets right on board. If what you have been doing so far to improve your marriage hasn't worked then you have little to lose trying something new.

How Good Is Your Math?

One more note about math and numbers. Are you and your spouse champion score keepers? You know. Keeping a mental running tab, like your marriage is some sort of competition. Here are some of the areas that couples find themselves keeping score over:

- who slept less
- who works more hours
- who does more chores
- who takes on more of the responsibilities with your children
- whose job/life is stressful in general

- who spends more "free time" hanging out with their friends or pursuing their hobbies
- who spends more of the disposable income (or who racks up more of the debt)
- which spouse's family you spend more time with

Here's the danger with keeping score. It turns your marriage into some sort of competition. And in a competition someone has to win. And in a marriage, if one person is winning, you are BOTH losing.

Things To Do Today

1. Understand that he first step in improving your day to day relationship with your spouse has to do with your mindset.
2. Recognize that you are 50% of your marriage and make a commitment to spend the next 30 days trying to change the "energy" in your relationship.
3. Decide to throw away the score sheet for 30 days. You plan on being married a long time, right? Call it a 30 day experiment.

I know this is the most vague and maybe "wishy washy" strategies that I am going to suggest in the book. But it is the best place to start. If you need to start with something more concrete and less reflective then just skip to another step. There are 9 more - something will resonate.

Chapter 2 - Focus on What You Want

So this step starts with an exercise. Take out a piece if paper. Write down 10 reasons you do not want your marriage to wither away from neglect. If you are reading this on the go and can't get to piece of paper, don't skip this step. Take some time to reflect. Give me 10 reasons you want your marriage to work. Go. I'm putting in numbers now to use up some space. Don't skip to the next page without doing the exercise or you'll be cheating yourself out of a powerful experience. You won't be cheating me. I already know pretty much how this is going to go for you, if you are like the majority of people.

Reasons I Want To Fix My Marriage

1

2

3

4

5

6

7

8

9

10

.

.

.

.

.

.

. come on.....do the exercise :)

.

.

.

.

.

OK. I'm going to take a guess at some of the items on your list. Off the top of my head here are some things that are probably sounding familiar.

Reasons You Want Your Marriage To Work

- You don't want your children to come form a "broken home".
- Divorce and having two households is really expensive. You need financial security.
- It's too hard to start all over at your age.
- You don't want to feel like you failed.

- You would be embarrassed about what your family, friends and church would think about you giving up on your marriage.
- You don't want to grow old alone.
- You don't want to have to raise your children alone.
- You don't want your ex spouse's new partner to have any part in raising your children.
- Almost everyone you know who is divorced lost their house and their savings.
- You want to know that if push comes to shove and you get really sick you are not alone - someone will be there to drive you to chemo and hold the bucket.

Do any of these items sound familiar? Probably so.

Here's the problem with this list. It's all about things that you DON'T WANT to happen. They are about things you want to move AWAY from. (Note, the list wasn't named "Reasons You Don't Want To Get Divorced").

Thinking about what we don't want is a very damaging habit. It is particularly prevalent in our culture and for most people it is a chronic way of thinking. Focusing on what you don't want and what you don't have is a really bad habit to get into and a very hard habit to break.

You are probably familiar with the basic idea that "like attracts like". It's the idea that focusing on positive things brings positive results whereas focusing on negative things brings negative results. It's the premise behind a "bad hair day" (you start the day off wrong and lo and behold if the whole day doesn't go a negative way) and self-fulfilling prophecies (if you tell yourself often enough that you are stupid and make bad decisions then no doubt you will live up to your own lack of expectations).

So it is important to develop the habit of focusing on what you DO WANT, things that you want to MOVE TOWARDS, not move away from.

As well as being resourceful, focusing on what you want is simply more pleasurable than focusing on what you don't.

I am an elementary school teacher. If you've spent any time in a classroom you know that the more relaxed, happier and more effective teachers are the ones who make a habit of praising and rewarding positive behavior. For example it's more pleasant to spend your day saying things such as "I love the way Jacob raised his hand to answer the question!" as opposed to "Johnny, don't just blurt out the answer - raise your hand!" From experience I can tell you that the positively phrased comments usually deliver better results and produce a better environment and a happier day for everyone involved.

How does this apply to your relationship with your spouse?

First, get very clear in your mind about the relationship that you DO want. Stop thinking about how you are bored, under appreciated or over stressed. Go back to your teenage fantasy years of when you dreamed of what getting married and living "happily ever after" looked like. Laughing as you and your spouse cook and eat together. Walking hand in hand as you walk the dog or take the children to school. Cuddling as you watch the sunset on the beach. Whatever "Hallmark" moment a great relationship would look like to you is the image you should put in your mind and the image to which you should aspire.

I have no idea what your ideal, perfect relationship looks like, but you should. That image should not be buried so far behind the images of all the ways your spouse irritates you that you can no longer access it.

One of the problems with our society is that the media loves to focus on negative things. Happy doesn't sell, apparently. Drama, conflict and bad news does. So when every tabloid is covered with stories of famous people caught cheating and celebrity "break ups" it's easy to get caught up in the notion that relationships never work out in the long run.

I have been reading and studying material in the relationship field for many years. In the past 10 years in the United States the divorce rate in first marriages has averaged around 50%. That's what we always hear, "50% of marriages end in divorce". Well, that means that in 50% of marriages, for better or worse, people hang in there and make their marriage work. 50% of first marriages DON'T end in divorce, that's what you want to focus on.

So with focusing on what we don't want being such a chronic way of thinking in our culture, what are some things you can do to focus on what you do want out of your marriage?

Here is a very tangible list of action items. Committing to doing at least one today would be a good place to start.

Things To Do Today

1. Take an inventory of your peer group. When you spend time with other couples, what is the dynamic of their relationship? Do you spend time primarily with couples who bicker, complain and who may be struggling with their own marriage problems? Or do you gravitate towards couples who seem happy and supportive of each other and like to have fun? See if maybe it would be more productive for you to spend more time around "positive" couples in your family and friend groups.

2. Create a positive image in your mind of what you want your relationship with your spouse to look like. Do whatever you can do to keep that image in your head as often as possible. This could include :

- Writing it down (make sure you use positive phrasing! For example, "we are always supportive of each other when dealing with our children" as opposed to "we don't undermine each other's authority in front of the children")

- Another powerful strategy could be to make a "vision board" or collage of photos of your favorite moments together as well as pictures of couples from magazines doing things that you would love to do (dancing on the beach! Holding hands while snorkeling...insert your Hallmark moment here!)

- Make a **"positive marriage vision movie"** and commit to watching it at least once a day. A simple short movie made of positive statements and images, set to inspiring music, just to put you in a positive frame of mind and feel good. You can easily make one using a presentation software and inserting your own favorite photos or stock photos from internet sites such as Dreamstime or Fotolia. Making a positive vision movie is a very pleasant way to spend an evening. You don't need to share it with your spouse if you don't want to. It's for you. Save it as a movie and watch it on your ipod during your lunch break or when waiting for the kids to finish soccer. It's just 5 minutes of

happiness and focusing on what you want. Just
simple affirmations and photos will work for
example,
"my spouse makes me laugh",
"I feel treasured and appreciated every day".

You can hop over to the OneNewHabit.com website
for an example. If the prospect of making a movie
seems too much for you, just watch mine. And it
would be a more resourceful way to spend 5
minutes than reading the tabloids about the most
recent celebrity break up scandal. You will find it
under the "Book Resources" tab.

Chapter 3 - Is It Time To Unplug?

Is Modern Technology Killing Your Marriage?

Do you know that 75% of surveyed couples who tried traditional marriage counseling reported that it had done very little to improve their marriage?

Have you ever tried it? Traditional marriage counseling has many limitations: it's expensive, time consuming, requires the participation of both parties and, for some, is received with the equivalent enthusiasm as the prospect of a dental root canal. I mean, who really wants to go hash out their dirty laundry and past and current problems in front of a stranger?

From my own experience I can tell you that one of the biggest problems with traditional marriage counseling is its strong focus on communication techniques. Most of traditional marriage counseling focuses on teaching couples "active listening" techniques. You know, mirroring back the words that your spouse has said to acknowledge that you have "heard them" and validate how they feel. Using "appropriate assertiveness" techniques and "I feel" statements to express yourself in a non-threatening and non accusatory manner.

With a great deal of certainty I can tell you that the problem with communicating with my husband when we were having problems was not that he didn't understand what I was saying and how I was feeling. It was that he DIDN'T CARE. *What was lacking from our marriage was not communication but connection.*

Experts have speculated how the internet has been "bad" for some marriages. They cite examples of couples who struggle with online shopping and gambling addictions or pornography addictions. Another area of concern is the ease with which on line chat rooms and social media sites have made it possible for people to engage in "virtual" or "emotional affairs" without ever getting out of their lazy chairs or their office. However, I believe that the real relationship killing potential with modern technology lies in another area - e-mail and text messaging.

Now, if you travel for business and you just booked a flight that your spouse needs to know about, go ahead and e-mail them the itinerary. If your child's soccer coach sends you an itinerary of the season's practice schedules, games and locations then likewise, hit "forward". But other than that, you should not be e-mailing your spouse. Seriously. Stop it. It's a really bad habit. E-mails are great for business and efficiently communicating things to groups of people, or people with whom you actually prefer not to have a conversation. If they have become your primary source of communicating with your spouse then you have a problem.

Regarding text messaging. Again, text messaging is a great tool. I especially love being able to text message my teenage children and keep up with their whereabouts. While it can seem "uncool" to talk to your mom on the phone, any teenager can respond to her text without fear of ridicule (who's to say you are not simply "Tweeting"?). Even in a marriage texting can have a useful function. "I'm running late, can you pick up the kids?" or "grab some milk when you're at the store, please" are all legitimate practical uses of your smart phone. Texting can be a great way to keep in touch when traveling away from your spouse or a nice way to reach and and "touch" them when they are working and a phone call would be inappropriate.

However, texting should not be your primary source of communication. You do not want to run the risk of your marriage deteriorating into a long list of delegated tasks. Too much of 'I'll do this, you do that" and suddenly your spouse is your assistant just helping you get through all the combined responsibilities of your day. When my own marriage was in a very bad state I used to joke how great texting was. It afforded the opportunity to communicate without ever having to actually talk and without that awkward moment at the end of a phone call when we were supposed to say "love you!" before you hanging up. I am hoping that doesn't sound painfully familiar to you.

Honor Your Bedroom As A Technology Free Haven

Many relationship counselors caution against having a television in your bedroom. Falling sleep watching television takes away opportunities for conversation and intimacy. It's great to think that you and your spouse will snuggle in bed together watching a romantic comedy. But more likely what happens is that you fall into a habit where you have separate bed times with one person watching something on the television downstairs while the other retreats to the bedroom to watch something else.

What about cell phones? Having your phone as a bedside companion can also be a bad habit. Do you really need to check Facebook last thing before you fall asleep? Ending the day and falling asleep next to the person you love is a very sacred part of marriage. It is an intimate act that you uniquely share with your partner.

Whether or not your end of day rituals include cuddling, being intimate or touching, they should at least involve some quiet talk and reflection. There is no legitimate reason to check your e-mails last thing before you go to sleep. Probably that notification sound on your phone is just some vendor sending you a sales e-mail. It has no business being in bed with you and the person you love.

Things To Do Today

1. For the whole day, try to keep a running track in your head or on a scrap of paper of what your primary mode of communication with your spouse is. Have you fallen into some bad habits?

2. Any time that you think about sending your spouse an e-mail pause and think. Is there a more personal way to communicate what you need to say?

3. Make sure that for every 2 super practical, essential texts you send your spouse you send them at least one unexpected simple "I love you", "I'm excited to see you later" or even something flirty.

4. Extra credit, go "old school" and write your spouse a love note. It needn't be a long letter. Just a quick note that you stick on their car seat or in their purse for them to find later. Something to give them an unexpected smile and make them feel cherished.

Chapter 4 - Do You Need A Purple Bracelet?

Here's what I learned in Therapy 101: "first come the thoughts, then come the feelings, then come the actions". Basically, we act a certain way because we feel a certain way, we feel a certain way because we are thinking something. So what are you thinking about when it comes to your marriage? Everything that's wrong with it?

Let's get back to our 80/20 principle. Is 20% of your spouse's behavior consuming 80% of your emotional energy?

Really think about this for a minute. Although it may seem some days like everything your spouse does gets on your nerves, it is probably less than 20% of their overall behavior that is irritating. Yet in your mind and your conversations with others, it is this 20% of behavior that gets all the air time. It circles back to the principle of focusing on what you want.

Now I'm not suggesting that you adopt my teacher tone and condescend to your spouse. I can't imagine that hearing "honey, I love the way you put down the toilet seat when you are done in the bathroom!" or "honey, I love the way you always wash the dishes right after dinner and don't let them pile up in the sink" will go over too well. However, making a solid decision to just stop talking about the things your spouse does that bother you will go over very well. Truly, it will probably go a long way to clearing up half of the tension and unspoken irritation that you may have lingering between you.

So what would the decision to "just stop talking about it" look like? It's pretty simple actually.

First, no more nagging. If nagging your spouse about the stuff they do that bothers you would make them change their behavior, they would have done it already. You should know by now that you cannot make someone change their behavior, only they can do that. Obviously nagging and complaining about your spouse's behavior hasn't changed the situation so far. So while you cannot change their behavior, you CAN change the way you react to it. And the best change you can make is just to stop reacting to it. (Now the obvious exclusion to this is any kind of dangerous behavior. Seriously dangerous behavior is going to need the intervention and support of professionals and so nagging is not going to make an impact either.)

I am not suggesting that if you stop talking about your spouse's irritating ways those habits will magically evaporate. But I am pointing out that all the energy you may be putting into complaining about that behavior, and focusing on what you don't want, is only making things worse and is not doing anything to contribute to good feelings and the vitality of your marriage.

So, that's first. Stop talking to your spouse about what they do that bothers you.

The second step may be harder for some people (sorry to admit, probably the women reading this book). And that step is to just stop talking about these irritations at all. To anyone. Stop complaining about your spouse's behavior to your friends, your co-workers, your family, your children (yikes!) and your hairdresser.

Men, you are not off the hook either. This means no more rolling of the eyes and joking about your wife being "high maintenance" to your friends and co-workers either. No more jokes about the old "ball and chain". While you think you might be "venting" and commiserating with your friends, what you are actually doing is just complaining. It is injecting negative energy into your relationship and in the long run does nothing to make you feel any better.

So what's the purple bracelet about?

Years ago on the Oprah show there was a pastor who had challenged his congregation to stop complaining about anything for 21 days. The idea was that it takes 21 days to break a habit, or make a new healthy one. He gave his congregation all a purple plastic bracelet. The idea is to start the day wearing the bracelet on one wrist, and if you complain during the day, to move it to the other wrist. The goal, of course, being to go 21 days without moving the bracelet. Every day that you move the bracelet you have to start from scratch. To date, more than 10 million bracelets have been distributed worldwide from the www.acomplaintfreeworld.org website. The site is fun and also has a Hall of Fame of all the people who have successfully completed the challenge (spoiler alert, the list of people is WAY less than 10 million!)

Things To Do Today

1. Do you need a constant visual reminder not to complain about your spouse to anyone? It might be time to order a bracelet (they're free). Visit www.acomplaintfreeworld.org

2. If a bracelet does not appeal to you, any way you choose to track your progress is fine. The complaint free world website also has a downloadable widget for your smart phone for the more technological minded folks. Heck, tie a piece of string around your finger if it will help you remember.

3. The most important thing to do is just to make the decision to stop talking about the things your spouse does that irritate you. We all seem to have no shortage of family members and friends who are willing to throw a "pity party" or sit around and "admire the problems" of our unhappy marriages. In reality, very few are truly qualified to give impartial, effective advice to help you improve the situation. So

just stop talking. That's it. And if you find that you have nothing else to talk about with your friends, then it might be time to reassess your peer group. Sorry if that sounds unduly harsh, but it may be the truth.

Chapter 5 - What's On Your List?

Did you get out of bed this morning with the express intention of getting frustrated by your kids? Of course not! Did you do it anyway? Probably. (Hey, I have teenagers in the house. Maybe my experience is different from yours but I doubt it.)

It's probably the same with your spouse. Don't assume they got out of bed thinking they wanted to spend their day irritating, frustrating and disappointing you. Maybe they did anyway, but assume the best intentions.

The reality is probably that your spouse is also not thoroughly thrilled with the state of your marriage. In which event anything YOU do to put some good energy back into it will be very well received and will be more likely to illicit some positive changes from your spouse.

Take out a piece of paper or open a text file and start listing everything you appreciate about your husband or wife. Start with the stuff that is probably huge, but that you have started to take for granted. Are they reliable? Do they get up and go to work every day? Do they come home every night? Do they work hard to make sure your children's needs are taken care off? Do they keep the house clean and food in the fridge and clean laundry in your drawer?

Maybe at first it will be hard to think of things. Keep that piece of paper or list handy. Every day for 30 days find at least 5 things that your spouse did that day that you appreciated. Even if it was only take out the trash and be polite to your mom when they answered the phone. Start digging back to the beginning of your relationship. List all the kind, fun things they did for you.

HERE'S THE KEY CONCEPT AGAIN, BY COMMITTING TO THIS EXERCISE YOU ARE FOCUSING ON WHAT YOU WANT, NOT ON WHAT YOU DON'T WANT.

This will change the energy in your thoughts about your spouse and your marriage. If you change the thoughts, chances are you can change the feelings. And then your actions will change. If your actions change, so will your spouses.

Now the other important part of this exercise is to share some of these thoughts with your spouse. Let me explain why.

I have spent a lot of time to reading and researching theories and studies on marriage, attraction and relationships. Time and time again much of the research always ends up with the same findings: women have a need to feel appreciated and men have a need to feel respected and admired.

For example, in his book The Truth About Cheating M.Gary Neuman shocked many people with his findings about male infidelity. Conventional stereotypes portray women as "straying" to fulfill an emotional need and men straying to fulfill a physical one (sex). However Neuman's research when interviewing men who cheated on their wives found that in 88% of the cases the new object of the man's affection was neither prettier, younger or in better shape than their wife. In the majority of cases men said they had strayed because they felt lonely in their marriage, were lacking attention from their wives and had a need to feel admired. This is why the stereotype of the man who cheats with his secretary persists with the subordinate presumably "looking up" to and admiring their boss. Not necessarily because she is younger and cuter and comes to work all made and dressed up, as opposed to walking around the house in her "comfy pants".

So at the end of the day it becomes vitally important to communicate to your spouse that they are appreciated and admired. It doesn't take much to do this. See below.

Things To Do Today

1. Start your list of things that you appreciate and enjoy about your spouse. Commit to add to the list every day for 30 days.

2. Choose one thing to share with your spouse today. Write them a quick note or send them an unexpected text with just a simple, honest

sentiment. Examples could be "I admire the way you always work so hard for our family without ever complaining. Thank you" or "I really appreciate how hard you work to make sure the kids look clean and neat when they leave the house in the morning. Thank you". These are all things that should not be taken for granted.

Chapter 6 - Laughing Yoga, Anyone?

Am I crazy? It may seem like a strange suggestion for a book on improving your marriage but in this step I am suggesting putting your marital problems on the back burner for a while. Hear me out on this.

Remember when you first got married and you couldn't wait to get home from work to be with your spouse? It didn't matter what was for dinner or what was on TV, you were just happy to come home and be together. Do you and your spouse still feel that way now? When was the last time either of you were the bright spot in each other's day? It's probably been a while.

Sharing a life with another person is full of a multitude of responsibilities. There are bills to be paid, lawns to be mowed, houses to be kept clean, children to raise, carpool to drive and aging parents to be attended to. And yet a marriage should not essentially be a job share.

You married your spouse because of the connection you felt to them on many levels. When marriages are struggling it is most often because that connection is dwindling or has become buried under a multitude of shared tasks, poor relationship habits and small annoyances. The best thing that you can do for your marriage is to try and regain that connection. And that's not going to be done by discussing your problems.

How can you reconnect?

Well, first you need some uninterrupted time together. Every marriage counselor out there will recommend that you have a standing "date night". If you haven't been on a date with your spouse for a while, get on it! Remember the classic "date night" rules - no talking about finances, children or your problems. Just like when you first dated, the focus should be on learning about each other and having fun.

Maybe you can recreate some of your first, fun dates (when was the last time you went bowling or miniature golfing?) If your conversation has gone stale over the years, you need to dig out some of your old date questions. You might think you know everything you need to know about your spouse. Maybe you don't, or maybe the answer to some of those questions has changed over the years. When was the last time you asked your spouse about their goals, their hopes, their fears? You should still have dreams together that go beyond the day to day mundane goals of getting through the month with enough money to pay all the bills. Ask your spouse, "if you could earn "x" amount (whatever number you could live comfortable on) a month doing whatever you wanted, what would you do?" Maybe the answer will surprise you.

If you do have regular dates, have they gone stale? Going to a movie is fun, but unless you plan on playing footsie it doesn't afford much opportunity for intimate conversation. Again, try something fun or new. Laughing yoga class not your style? Maybe you and your spouse could just watch some "laughing yoga" videos on Youtube together. Silly? I dare you not to laugh, even if for the wrong reasons. Even staying home can be fun if you get in the right mind frame.

Dates are nice, but even more important is finding time to connect in your "regular" life together.

Have you fallen into bad relationship habits that might include:

- different bed times
- different bed rooms
- watching TV in different room
- one of you always doing household chores inside while the other always works outside (yard work, fiddling in the garage)

Basically, anything you can do to spend more time actually together is going to boost your opportunities to connect.

Maybe suggest that one weekend you will both work together to clean the house then go outside and do yard work together. Or agree to have 15 minutes of "quiet time" together without TV or computers after the children are put to bed.

This is a strategy I used for years when putting my children to bed. We always ended our day with "happy thoughts". We all told each other the 3 best parts of our day. I saw Michelle Obama being interviewed recently and her version of this was called 'the rose and the thorn". Daily, around the dinner table, the first family talks about the best part of their day (the rose) and the worst part (the thorn). I would suggest keeping things upbeat. So maybe just get into a habit of asking your spouse "what was the best part of your day today?" or "who was someone who made a positive difference in your day today?" Any conversation that keeps you connected.

Let me stress this one more time. You need to focus on having fun with your spouse. Any way you can find to be playful, silly or even flirtatious is good. How about busting out the children's video games when they go to bed? Or playing with some of their toys? These are things you don't need to leave the house to do if finding a babysitter is stressful or a financial hardship. You know the saying "the family who plays together, stays together?". Turns out it's true.

Things To Do Today

1. Take some time to determine how much time you have spent alone with your spouse during the last week. There are 168 hours in a week - is the number you came up with really small? Make a commitment to double that "alone" time this week.

2. Also ponder this question. How did you spend that time together? Were you having fun? Were you engaged in activities and conversations that were based on connection or just the communicating of facts and delegation of chores?

3. Plan one date for the upcoming week. Take responsibility for making all the arrangements. Present is as a fun escape, not as a negative. "We never go out!" or "We need to do this" are complaints. We gave up complaining in the last chapter, right?

Chapter 7 - Where Do You Crave To Be Touched?

No book on improving your marriage would be complete without addressing the issue of intimacy and passion. Intimacy could include having sexual relations with your spouse. If sexual intimacy has been lacking from your marriage for a while and you feel that you have real issues that need to be addressed before you can get sex back on the menu, then just getting some sort of intimate hugging, cuddling back in your marriage is an essential goal.

If you are currently sexually active with your spouse but you feel that your sex life has gotten a little stale, routine and "going through the motions", then your goal is to inject some passion and excitement back into your love making.

Whatever your goal, start with this idea is mind. Touching in a marriage is REALLY important. Intimacy is really important. If you think that it is not then not only are you kidding yourself, but you are cheating yourself and your partner out of one of the unique facets of a marriage.

I do not have the experience or expertise to advise you if there are serious problems that you face in this area. If you or your spouse have unresolved issues around physical intimacy then it would be appropriate to consult a professional. That's not me. However, the majority of problems that couples face in this department are not due to major unresolved issues. Most problems are the result of "life" just getting in the way and people falling into bad relationship habits. With the constant barrage of responsibilities that demand your time and energy, intimacy simply ceases to be a top priority.

First, it is important to recognize that all relationships go through cycles. When you were first a couple a combination of hormones and those little understood things called pheromones were all kicking into high gear. In all likelihood you could hardly keep your hands off each other. It is inevitable that this stage of a relationship wanes a little after the first few years. That is not to say that couples cannot and should not enjoy a healthy, satisfying life of love making together that spans the entire length of their marriage, even when the initial degree of urgency has gone. But when the reality of married life sets in, other priorities just seem to take over. And this is when unhealthy relationship habits form.

So what are some unhealthy habits that couples fall into that are "passion killers"? Take a look at this list and see how many apply to your marriage.

- separate bed times or beds.

- allowing your children to sleep in your bed with you.

- electronics in the bedroom (TV, cell phone, lap tops).

- assuming that intimacy can only happen at night. Let's face it by the time you get to bed chances are you are physically and mentally exhausted and you've got very little left to give.

- lack of focus on your appearance and best grooming when at home. Obviously sweats and pajamas are comfortable and relaxing but they probably don't do much to ignite passion.

- allowing your love making to fall into a predictable routine.

- lack of intimacy, touching, hand holding and cuddling in general and then suddenly expecting your spouse to be interested in having sex with you.

- fulfilling your needs alone by reading smutty novels (are there any women left who haven't read Fifty Shades of Gray?) or watching TV or internet porn.

So assuming that you would like to get intimacy and passion back on the agenda, where should you start?

Let me quote an Italian proverb that says "l'appetito vien mangiando". Basically this translates to "your appetite comes from eating". Let me explain.

Years ago, before Dr. Phil and the likes were on the television, people relied on radio talk shows for advice. One of the most popular pioneers in dispensing advice on sexual issues was a German/American sex therapist Dr. Ruth Westheimer (commonly known as "Dr. Ruth"). One day back in the 1980s when I was listening to her show a woman called in and said she had lost her desire to have sex with her husband and wanted to know what she should do about it. Dr. Ruth's plain answer was "have sex with him". The idea being, don't wait until you feel turned on to initiate sex, initiate sex and the feelings of arousal will come. The appetite will come when you are eating. Or as Nike would say, "just do it!"

It's not that difficult. Set the stage by ensuring you have uninterrupted time alone with your spouse, make an effort to look your best, maybe open a bottle of wine. Be the one to initiate touching and cuddling and see where it ends up.

Of course, for many people (especially women), sexual intimacy is not possible without emotional intimacy. If you have been working on some of the other strategies in this book that focus on reconnecting emotionally with your spouse and having fun, then it is going to be a lot easier to reconnect in the physical department. You might not want to jump straight to third base or "home run".

If any type of touching has been absent from your marriage for a while, then the focus should be on just getting some sort of touching back in your routine interactions. Make a commitment to "touch" your spouse at least twice a day. Any kind of touching will do. Some non-threatening examples would be:

- touching your spouse's arm when you laugh

- snuggling close to your spouse on the couch

- taking their hand and holding it when you walk somewhere

- rubbing their neck or shoulders while they are sitting at their desk or washing dishes

- giving a foot or back rub

- playing with your spouse's hair when you talk last thing at night

- offering to run them a bath and then offering to wash their back or their hair

- kissing. Yes, a good old fashioned kiss with no expectation of it leading to anything else

If you are currently having a sexual relationship with your spouse but you want to mix things up a bit or break out of the routine you could try this exercise. It was featured on an episode of Oprah with sex therapist Dr. Laura Berman.

Foreplay Preference Exercise

In this exercise you provide your partner with a blank outline of a human body and ask them to number the areas of the body that they would like to be touched in priority order. For example, someone might put #1 on the ear, #2 on the lips, #3 on the nipples etc. The idea behind this exercise is to test your knowledge of your partner's arousal preferences. Couples on the Oprah show were surprised to see their partner's results. Some women were surprised to find that their husband did not in fact want them to launch straight to the genital region. This type of exercise can be an easy and non-threatening way to start a discussion or foreplay session for couples who would feel awkward actually talking about sex. Maybe after years of the same sexual routine you would feel uncomfortable suddenly mentioning "actually I don't really like it when you touch me there". This exercise provides a non-judgmental way of approaching the subject.

Things To Do Today

1. If you are not currently making love to your spouse, commit to touching them at least 2

times a day for 2 weeks. Then see where things lead.

2. If you are currently having sex, mix things up a bit and try the Foreplay Preference Exercise.

3. Whether or not you are currently being intimate **DO THIS** : When your spouse comes home tonight, drop everything you are doing and go greet them with a 5 second kiss. If you are the one who gets home later, when you come in the door go find your spouse straight away and greet them with a 5 second kiss. It doesn't matter if the kids, the dog or your parents are watching. Just do it.

4. Make time to watch either of these 2 videos. They are based on the excellent research of renowned couples therapist Esther Perel and her 2002 best seller <u>Mating In Captivity</u>. Perel's research and writing centers around how to sustain desire in a long term relationship. Her book is excellent and her research fascinating, but beyond the scope of what you have signed up to read here. So there are 2 video links here (if you don't have time now or are not reading on a web enabled device I include the links at the end of the book again).

    <u>THIS LINK</u> is a 20 minute live recording of her famous TED Talk on the subject. If you

are reading a paperback version of this book, not electronic, go to www.OneNewHabit.com and see the tab "Book Resources" where I have embedded all the videos.

THIS LINK is a 5 minute YouTube of an interview segment she gave on The Today Show in Australia about her work. Again, If you are reading a paperback version of this book, not electronic, go to www.OneNewHabit.com and see the tab "Book Resources" where I have embedded all the videos.

Chapter 8 - Pick A Chore, Any Chore

Maintaining a household on a day to day basis is a chore - there are a thousand little jobs that need to be tended to. Cleaning, organizing, shopping, cooking, laundry, homework help, driving kids to activities, paying bills, mowing lawns, raking leaves, taking out trash...the list goes on and on. When you are exhausted from all that you do it might sometimes feel like you bear the brunt of the work, and that you are under appreciated. If you really DO take care of most of the work, without complaining and waiting for a little appreciation, then you need to rethink this. The world does not need any more martyrs. Ask your spouse kindly to do their fair share, and present them with specific requests as opposed to just complaining "you never do anything!" (We gave up complaining in Chapter 4, as you may recall).

However, in the majority of marriages, there is probably a pretty equal distribution of labor. Take some time to objectively think about the duties your spouse routinely takes care of. As a pure gesture of goodwill and to try and change the energy in your marriage, is there something you could do off your spouse's list today as a surprise? And (here's the kicker) not even mention it? Don't do the chore with any expectation of being thanked or in the hope that your spouse will do one of your chores. Do this chore just as a random act of kindness, a little something just to make your spouse's day go a little easier. Just do it and see what happens. Worst case scenario, your spouse won't notice. But I am guessing they will and it will go a long way to put a deposit in their "emotional bank account".

This is a good time to talk about:

Emotional Bank Accounts

You may have heard that "love is a verb". You remember verbs from school, they're the "doing" words. Run, jump, eat, stand, talk, work, complain and sleep are all examples of verbs, things that you do. So it turns out that love is something that we do, rather than something that we feel. When we act lovingly towards someone, with a million small deeds and thoughts and we receive the way we feel when we are around them, that's when love happens.

The idea of an emotional bank account is like that of a regular bank account that deals with debits and credits. We receive deposits when someone does something loving towards us, and withdrawals when we we do something in return or something is "taken".

As with any bank account, you need to deposit into your spouse's emotional bank account before you can make a withdrawal.

Many marriages start to feel great tension and fall apart when there is a real (or perceived) inequity in the amount of deposits versus the withdrawals.

When one partner starts to feel that the other is basically taking more than they are giving then the emotional bank account is severely in the red.

Any loving act, freely given, will put a deposit in their emotional bank account. This could be as simple as doing one of their chores for no particular reason, other than to lighten your spouse's load a little.

I am reminded of a chapter in Richard Carlson's excellent book <u>Don't Sweat The Small Stuff, And It's All Small Stuff</u>. The chapter is entitled "When in doubt whose turn it is to take out the trash, go ahead and take it out". At the end of the day a gesture of goodwill and just taking care of the task can be easier and more time effective than reminding or nagging your spouse to take out the trash.

Things To Do Today

1. Spend some time thinking about all of the responsibilities and chores that your spouse routinely takes care of. The idea is not to have a comparison chart (we also gave up "counting" right?) but to gain awareness that even though it sometimes feels as if you are the only one working hard to maintain the household, this is probably not true.

2. Pick one chore that you will do off your spouse's list today without telling them or expecting them to reciprocate. It can be

especially fun to pick a chore that goes against established gender based stereotypes. For example, should the wife always cook and the husband always mow the lawn?

3. Commit to TWO things today that you could do that would put a deposit in your spouse's emotional bank account.

Chapter 9 - Do You Fight Fair?

No long term, committed relationship can exist without some sort of conflict. Now one of the key concepts of this book is how the energy in your marriage needs to change and that you should stop constantly talking about your marriage problems. Even if you stop talking about problem areas, areas will still come up with your spouse on a day to day basis where you do not agree or you have seriously irritated each other. Chances are at some point before too long you are going to argue and learning to fight fair, in a way that strengthens and not damages a relationship, is important.

First, for those of you who say, "but we never argue" (yes, there are couples out there who say that). Not arguing or disagreeing is a really dangerous relationship habit. Even though this habit may have evolved for many legitimate reasons (for me, it was my determination never to have my parent's marriage, which was pretty full of fireworks) it is still a bad relationship habit.

Top relationship coach Mort Fertel notes in his excellent <u>Marriage Fitness Program</u> that "hate isn't the opposite of love, indifference is". If your marriage has deteriorated to the point where you can't even be bothered to argue then you really have a lot of work to do.

What constitutes fighting fair?

Stick to the topic at hand

Many couples will recognize that pattern of repeating the same argument over and over. Even if you start arguing about one thing, suddenly unresolved issues or old hurts that one partner is unwilling to let go get brought up. It can seem that instead of having maybe 10 arguments in the last 5 years, you've just the same argument 10 times. If there is an issue in your marriage that you have been unable to resolve thus far either decide it's a deal breaker or commit to stop arguing about it. Obviously arguing about it isn't going to resolve it. Is it something you are willing to end your marriage over? If not, then find a way to try and resolve it when you are both in a calmer state, not in the heat of battle.

Is the topic a deal breaker?

Again, is this something you are willing to end your marriage over? Sometimes couples argue over things that, in the whole scheme of things, are really pretty insignificant. Your spouse over spending, addiction and infidelity issues, bad parenting decisions...these are all legitimate issues. Who left the TV on all night or forgot to pick up milk are really not deal breakers. Like the expression says, "don't make mountains out of mole hills".

Never threaten to leave or get divorced

If you are seriously considering leaving the marriage and filing for divorce, sit and discuss this in a non heated moment. If you have ever uttered the words "I'm going to leave you!" and you haven't done it then it's an idle, childish threat and non productive. Making your partner feel insecure about the state of your marriage is not helpful. Don't do it.

Stop picking at scabs

By the time we are old enough to be in a mature relationship most of us have suffered through quite a bit of life. Regardless of how we grow up, poor or privileged, loved or neglected, no one gets to grow up unscathed. In all likelihood your spouse has some old psychological wounds that were inflicted somewhere along the way. Loving someone and confiding those wounds to them makes you vulnerable. You are probably privy to your spouse's wounds more than anyone else. It is a horrible breach of trust to pick at those wounds when you are angry and fighting. Probably your spouse also has some fresher wounds (self-inflicted or not) that occurred during the marriage. Wounds need to heal. To keep picking at them just delays the healing process. Picking at your spouse's vulnerable spot is not fighting fair.

Talk to your spouse directly about what is bothering you

Do not recruit your children into messengers in your private battles with your spouse. Even if you know better than to argue in front of your children (please say that you do) it is not fair to send them relaying messages when you and your spouse are in the "not talking" phase. Calmly explaining to your children that "mommy and daddy" have been disagreeing about some things and that you are sure the tension will subside soon when you work through it is fine. Bad mouthing your spouse and trying to get your children to side with you is emotional warfare, not fighting fair and bad parenting.

Likewise, do not drag your friends and family members into your quarrels. If your spouse has done something to upset you, or has a habit you want them to change, then discuss it with them directly. Do not resort to bringing the issues up in front of your family and friends, especially in the form of "teasing" or "just joking". Hostility and criticism masked as joking is passive aggressive behavior and unproductive at best. It can be deeply hurtful and damaging to your relationship. It also probably makes your friends and family uncomfortable.

Maybe lighten up on yourself and your position that you are never wrong

Most of the time agreeing with criticism makes it go away. If just once when your spouse tells you that you are stubborn you say, "you're right, I can be a little stubborn, I should look at that" that would pretty much end the discussion right there. Defending your self and hurling back a list of your spouse's real or perceived character flaws only escalates the situation. Before you know it you are picking at old scabs, and having the same argument you have had a hundred times. Acknowledging that there might be some truth to the criticism completely diffuses the situation.

Things To Do Today

1. Think of the last 3 or 4 arguments that you have had with your spouse. Do they always end up in the same place? List 2 ways that you could try and resolve this issue outside of an argument.

2. Resolve to delete the words "I'm going to leave" or "I'm going to divorce you" from your vocabulary. It's probably an idle threat even if that is how you feel in the heat of the moment. If you know in your heart that the issue you are arguing over is not a deal breaker and that it will blow over eventually, saying these words is only inflicting more damage.

Chapter 10 - Be Happy Anyway

When I had my first child I stumbled across a piece of advice called "The Paradoxical Rules of Parenting". I can't remember if someone gave it to me, or I found it in a magazine (we're talking pre-internet, here). Anyway, it was a list of ten paradoxes. I typed them up and they hung on my fridge for 16 years. Examples were, "Children won't always appreciate that you work hard and give them your best. Give them your best anyway" and "Children will want to stand on their own two feet and may fall. Let them stand on their own feet anyway". Paradox number 10 was this :

"Some days you may not feel a smile and a song in your heart. Smile and sing anyway".

Year after year, every time I looked at my fridge, number 10 seemed to be calling me. "Smile and sing anyway". Now with more than 20 years of reading and studying in the area of self-development under my belt it's still some of the best wisdom I have ever come across. As simple as that, "smile and sing anyway".

How will this transform your marriage?

First, recognize that you do have the ability to be happy regardless of the current or future state of your marriage. Now that's a short sentence but a profound concept.

Recognize that happiness is a state of consciousness, not a circumstance.

You simply cannot wait to be happy until your relationship with your spouse is improved, or you lose that last 15 pounds, or you get a better job, or your children grow more independent. You can only be happy now. It's a choice you have to make, and something you have to work on (some harder than others), not just wait for it to happen.

Please don't waste precious time thinking that you won't be happy until your life magically all "falls into place" one day. That day will never come. There will never be a day where everything is perfect and you have nothing to worry about. Well, maybe there will be one isolated day, when you go on vacation and turn off your cell phone, and enjoy awesome honeymoon type love making and amazing meals without worrying about the calorie count. But that will be one isolated day, or at best, a week. That's not your life. Your life is now, today, with all it's business, responsibilities and little frustrations. And you need to find a way to be happy regardless.

No one is responsible for your happiness accept you. Not your parents, not your children and certainly not your spouse. They can contribute to your happiness, they can influence it, but they are not responsible for it. So please recognize that finding a way to be happy now, yourself, is a really important goal for you.

How can you go about being happy?

Obviously this is a huge topic beyond the scope of this book. Luckily, there is a <u>One New Habit</u> book dedicated to the very subject of how to find joy and happiness in your everyday life. It is available on Amazon and comes with a free 40 page work book. More information can also be found at the end of this book. If you are reading a paperback version of this book just go to Amazon and search under my author name Grace Stevens and all of my books will appear. The book in question is called <u>The Happy Habit</u>.

In the meantime, here is a short list of things that you can at least start to work on with the goal of being happy in mind.

Take care of your body

Your mind, body and spirit are all connected. While there are beautiful stories out there of people who manage to be in a state of bliss despite the fact that their body is ravaged with disease, most of us just simply feel better when our body is working well. Simple things such as getting enough sleep, eating food that nourishes your body and keeping your body moving so that your joints aren't stiff can really help with your overall outlook. It is really hard to make time to look after yourself when you have so many other responsibilities on a day to day basis. But at the end of the day you are no use to your family when you are exhausted, grumpy and sick.

Make getting enough sleep a priority

An extra hour's sleep will do more for you than that hour of reruns and reality shows on television. Make preparing and eating healthy food a priority for you and your family. Our bodies were not designed to consume "fast food" in the car on the way from one activity to the next. Also find a way to exercise, even if it is just walking around the block a few times. As well as ensuring your body keeps working well, exercise releases endorphins. Endorphins are those chemicals that stimulate the parts of the brain that block pain and feel intense pleasure. Endorphins are good.

Do things that make you happy

When was the last time that you did something that really makes you happy? Of course a week long beach vacation sounds lovely. But on a day to day basis it's probably little things that add to your joy.

For me it can be cutting and arranging flowers from my garden, taking the time to write a hand written card to someone I love for no particular reason, or just riding my bike around the neighborhood early in the morning when it is cool and quiet.

When I find myself getting overly stressed and overwhelmed if I examine how I have been spending my time more often than not I will find that I have been neglecting to take a few minutes daily to connect to my joy. Take some time to reconnect with the little things that make you happy. A warm bath listening to music, rolling on the floor with your dog, a yoga class, polishing your car, having a pillow fight with your kids. It doesn't matter what it is. You need to find a way to get 10 minutes of happy time into your day, every day.

"Fake it til you make it"

Whenever I am feeling a little down and sorry for myself, I always hear my mother's voice saying "slap a little lipstick on, you'll feel better!" Can lipstick really make you feel better?

What many of us appreciate about being at home is that we can be comfortable and not have to impress others. Being able to relax in your own home is important. Personally, I can't wait to get home and kick off my heels. However, always being in "comfort mode" at home is not advisable. In reality, here's what "comfort mode" looks like. For women it's no make up, hair pulled back and sweats or (for those of you old enough to remember your mother in one) a housecoat. For men it's probably unshaven, unshowered, sweats and a baseball cap. Hardly the stuff of high romance and first dates.

Not only can being constantly scruffy around the house be unappealing to your spouse, it can also be detrimental to your mood. Let's be honest, we live in a culture that often equates poor mental health with poor hygiene. When you look at yourself in the mirror all scruffy and disheveled it's hard to feel good about yourself. Simply getting nicely cleaned up and dressed up and smiling can do a lot to boost your own spirits. Putting on the air of being happy and cheerful can be the first step in actually feeling that way. Fake it til you make it. Even of you don't feel significantly better, people around you will definitely appreciate it and react to you differently. This in turn can make a difference in your day.

Focusing on being happy should be a goal in itself for you. However, here's the added bonus. If you are happier YOUR MARRIAGE WILL IMPROVE.

Ask yourself this, do you prefer being around worn out, over stressed, short tempered people, or people who "smile and sing anyway"?

As well as being more fun to be around, your spouse will actually be more attracted to you if you are happy. All the research on attraction points to the fact that people are attracted to others who seem friendly, happy and self confident. People who have full lives and interests of their own, who seem "whole" and happy without needing another person to "complete" them are the people who get most of the attention in the dating world. One of the most honest internet dating profiles I ever saw was where a man listed as his requirements "you should be passionate about something. It doesn't matter what it is, as long as you are passionate about something".

In her research for her best-selling book <u>Mating In Captivity</u>, Esther Perel asks hundreds of couples "when do you feel most attracted toward your partner?". Most of the answers centered around seeing their partner "in their element", doing something that they loved or were admired for. Conversely, when she asked couples, "when do you feel most turned on and attractive", people said that when they felt most "alive" and involved in things that brought them passion is when they felt most desirable. So you see how important it is for your own desire and that of your partner for you to have rewarding, engaging pursuits of your own that make you happy.

One common complaint that comes up when marriages start to deteriorate is "what happened to the person I married?" Where did that confident, fun person with all those interests go? Are they sitting on the couch in their sweats watching football? Or are they overly involved in all of your children's activities, gaining all of their validation from your children's achievements? Is making the perfect cupcake the whole focus of their day?

Did you ever have one of those annoying friends who seemed to suddenly "ditch" you whenever they had a new boyfriend or girlfriend? Instead of having friends and interests of their own they would morph into some version of their dating partner, adopting all of their partner's interests and their partner's friends? How did those relationships pan out in the long run? I'm guessing they didn't.

Quite simply, people like to be around happy, fulfilled people. Don't wait for your marriage to improve to be happy. Find a way to be happy and you will find that your marriage can only benefit in a positive way.

Things To Do Today

1. Make a list of 5 simple things that give you joy. Look at your schedule and determine what can be changed to accommodate you doing at least one of these things for the next 5 days. Can you do them during your lunch hour at work? Can you do one instead of watching television? Only you can decide where your priorities lie.

2. Put your best foot forward. Whatever time your spouse spends with you today, make sure you are looking your best.

*** Extra credit, break out your best dating lingerie or underwear and see if they notice.

Conclusion

You've finished reading, now what are you going to do?

There are many simple strategies in this book. Note, I said "simple, not "easy". Changing the way we think, feel and act is no easy task. Reading this book is NOT going to change your marriage, but implementing these strategies will. Now comes the time to act. Which of these 10 things are you going to do today?

Stop press!

During the final days of me editing this book, renowned relationship expert John Gottman published a new book called <u>What Makes Love Last</u>. For over 25 years Dr. Gottman has been famous for his "love lab" experiments and expertise in the area of research as well as clinical practice with marriages and families. He has been featured on CNN, 60 Minutes and is a repeated New York Times best seller. Basically, when it comes to marriages and relationships, he knows his stuff. Here is what he says in introducing his book:

"You have to actively cherish your partner's positive qualities and think how lucky you are to have this person in your life. And let them know that they really are special. If both parties do this, the relationship can last forever".

Exactly. Please go do that today. I wish you the best of luck!

Excellent Resources

Remember, this book is for people who need help to **recharge** their marriage. If your marriage is suffering from serious problems such as addiction or abuse, please get professional help.

If you or anyone you know is suffering from domestic abuse you are NOT alone and there IS help out there.

For a copy of the Domestic Violence Awareness Handbook visit:

http://www.dm.usda.gov/shmd/aware.htm

or call

National Domestic Violence Hotline 1-800-799-SAFE

Here is where you can find extra information on the books and research referenced in this book :

The Truth About Cheating - 2006, M. Gary Neuman

Available on Amazon

Don't Sweat The Small Stuff And It's All Small Stuff - 2002, Richard Carlson

Available on Amazon

<u>What Makes Love Last ? How To Build Trust And</u>
<u>Avoid Betrayal</u> - 2012, Dr. John Gottman
 Available on Amazon

<u>Mating In Captivity</u> - 2006, Esther Perel

Available on Amazon

For more information on Dr. Ruth Westheimer visit

<u>http://en.wikipedia.org/wiki/Ruth Westheimer</u>

For more information on Dr. Laura Berman visit

<u>http://en.wikipedia.org/wiki/Laura Berman</u>

To watch Esther Perel's famous TED Talk Click on
the image below. If not using a web enabled device
you can search "Esther Perel TED Talk 2008" and it
will be on the first page.

Esther Perel: The secret to desire in a long-term relationship

Also, this video is embedded on my website at www.OneNewHabit/BookResources

What if you need more help?

If your marriage needs MORE HELP than the scope of this short book, the best resource I have found on line is **The Marriage Fitness Program** by Mort Fertel. Mort is a top marriage and relationship coach and therapist and has worked successfully with thousands of couples. He has programs for all budgets, ranging from a DVD series to weekly tele-conference calls and even, for those in his area, in home coaching. His Lone Ranger program works especially well in situations where one spouse is trying to fix a marriage alone (i.e. their spouse is unwilling to try counseling).

You can find FREE marriage assessments at his Marriage Fitness site at www.marriagemax.com

For a FREE 14 part e-course you can visit www.OneNewHabit.com/marriage-gift

THANK YOU for buying this book. Book reviews are very important to me and to Amazon. They help us make books and your buying and reading experience better. If you liked this book, I would REALLY appreciate it if you take a few moments to review this book on Amazon.

Things to do NOW :)

Leave a review for this book on Amazon. com

LIKE my Facebook page and help create a community of fans commenting on how they are using these strategies. You'll get a little dose of happy in your FaceBook feed when you most need it. You can find it at : https://www.facebook.com/OneNewHabit

Check out other books in the One New Habit Series:

What people are saying about this book:

"While this is an "easy" read - the "simple" steps that the author outlines, and the questions she asks are truly thought-provoking. This is a quick and easy read that is loaded with facts, studies, and SIMPLE ways to get thinking about, and ACTING on your own path to happiness. The author's style is casual and informal - and very easy to read." Amazon 5 star ***** review

"What can I say? I LOVED this little book. The question you need to ask yourself is are you happy right now? If not, do you want to be happy? If you answered "YES" to that second question this is the book for you." Amazon 5 star ***** review

What people are saying about this book:

"Another great book from Grace Stevens! Love the ideas broken down into small to-do items. Makes the information easy to understand and accomplish....which is key for an Anti-Procrastination book. Grace includes interesting examples and links to Ted talks (which I love!). She includes several different ways of understanding her information, which is great for every type of learner. LOVE her books....can't wait for more!"

Amazon 5 star ***** review

"To my surprise I found not one but many habits I can do right away. As I read the book, I put it down to set my timer and do a 20 minute power cleaning, I was feeling motivated ;). I specially like all the resources provided at the end of the book!"

*Amazon 5 star ***** review*

About The Author

"Simple Strategies You Can Use Today To Transform Your Life"

Grace Stevens writes concise, practical self-help books in the topic of relationships. Relationships with your spouse, your friends, your children and also your relationship with yourself and the world around you (what most people refer to as "happiness").

In her book series <u>One New Habit</u> she breaks down seemingly overwhelming problems into simple, actionable steps that anyone can implement TODAY to improve their relationships and their life.

A self-confessed "self-help nerd," Grace's books combine a mixture of current research and practical examples and tips, all in an easy to read conversational tone.

Grace lived and studied in 4 countries before making California her home. When not reading or writing she can be found outside having fun with her two teenagers and many friends, or inside teaching young children to love learning and the importance of washing their hands. She may or may not be addicted to TED talks.

30920600R00044

Made in the USA
Lexington, KY
23 March 2014